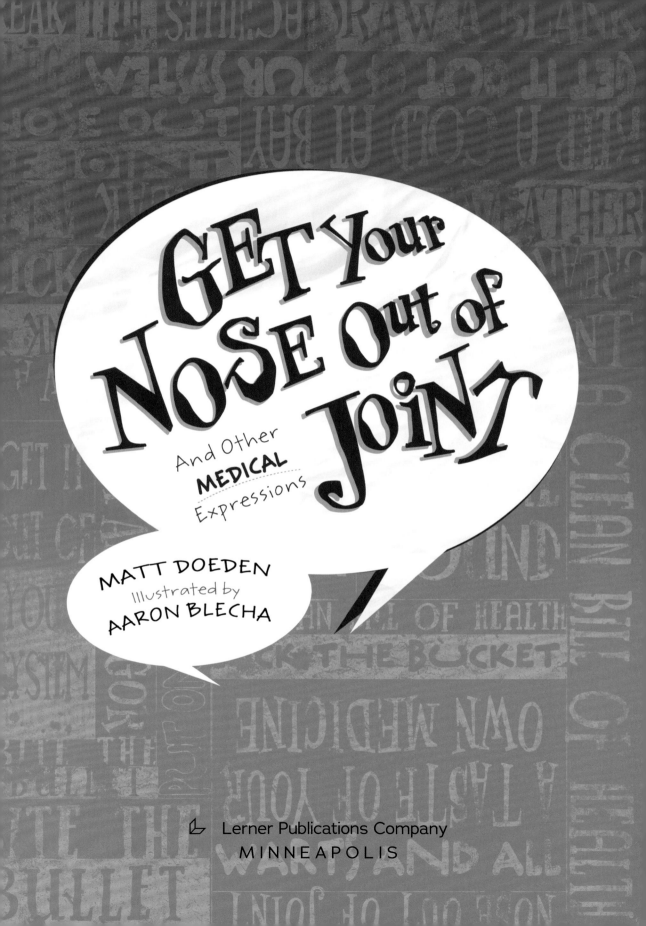

GET Your NOSE Out of JOINT

And Other MEDICAL Expressions

MATT DOEDEN

Illustrated by
AARON BLECHA

Lerner Publications Company
MINNEAPOLIS

Lerner Publications Company
A division of Lerner Publishing Group, Inc.
241 First Avenue North
Minneapolis, MN 55401 U.S.A.

Website address: www.lernerbooks.com

Library of Congress Cataloging-in-Publication Data

Doeden, Matt.
    Get your nose out of joint : and other medical
expressions / by Matt Doeden.
       p.   cm. — (It's just an expression)
    Includes index.
    ISBN 978-0-7613-8163-1 (lib. bdg. : alk. paper)
    1. English language—Idioms—Juvenile literature.
2. Figures of speech—Juvenile literature. I. Title.
PE1460.D68 2013
428.1—dc23   2011045097

Manufactured in the United States of America
1 – PC – 7/15/12

TABLE of CONTENTS

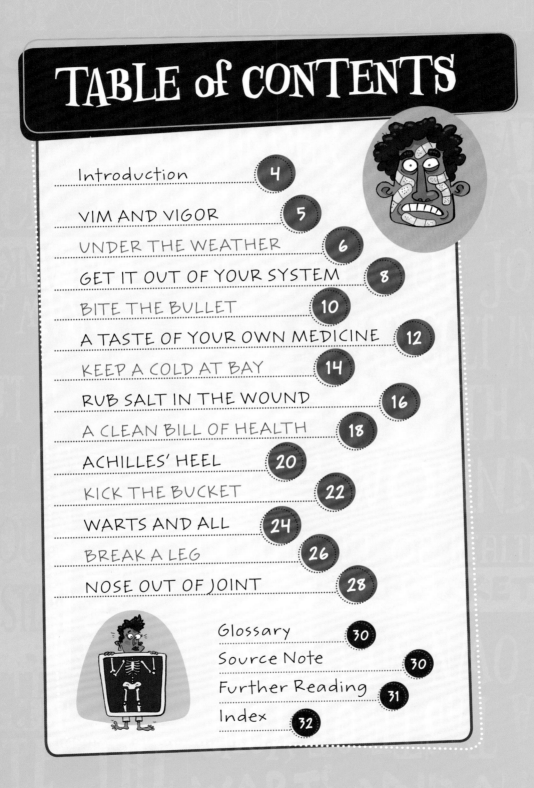

INTRODUCTION

"I don't think I can go to school today," Randall groaned as his mom told him to get out of bed. "I'm feeling **under the weather.**"

Randall's mom gave him a dirty look. "Last night when you stayed up late to play video games, you were full of **vim and vigor.** And don't you have a school party today?"

"Aww, Mom, you don't have to **rub salt in the wound,**" Randall said with a frown. He'd forgotten all about the party. *Darn*, he thought. *Remembering stuff always was my* **Achilles' heel.**

"Well, maybe I can go after all," he said. "I may not have **a clean bill of health,** but it's not like I'm about to **kick the bucket** or anything."

What are these two talking about? Buckets, bills, something called vim, and what may or may not be bad weather? Is this stuff supposed to make any sense? Yes! But only if you know your idioms. <u>Idioms are phrases that mean something different from what you might think they mean.</u> If you don't know what they mean, you may feel hopelessly lost. But if you **bite the bullet** and commit to learning all about them, they won't seem so confusing after all!

VIM and VIGOR

"I love our new football coach," T.J. told his uncle. "He's really full of vim and vigor."

Full of *what* and *what* now? Is vim and vigor the latest, greatest new offensive formation in football? It seems like usually when we say someone is full of something, it's not a good thing. So what gives?

When we say someone is full of vim and vigor, it's a compliment. It means that a person is healthy and full of enthusiasm. Those are great traits in a football coach. Or in a teacher or in a student or ... really, in just about anyone!

The origin of this expression is uncertain. But vim means "energy" and vigor means "health"— and the two words are pretty fun to say together. Just try saying them aloud. It might just be that someone used both these words to describe someone once, and the catchy phrase began to spread. But however this idiom got its start, a little vim and vigor in your life is never a bad thing!

This coach is full of vim and vigor. He's just raring to go!

UNDER the WEATHER

"Maria, where is your brother today?" asked Mr. Stevens, the band director. "I'm short one saxophone player."

This band is down one saxophone player. Why? The player is under the weather.

"He's not coming," said Maria. "He's feeling a little under the weather."

Say what? Maybe it's sunny outside or rainy or snowing ... or whatever. No matter what the weather, it seems hard to imagine being under it, over it, off to the side of it, or anything but *in* it.

People love to talk about the weather. But in this case, they're talking about something completely different. **If someone is under the weather, he or she is feeling sick.**

The whole city of Tucson, Arizona, is under the weather in this picture ... literally!

That person's not really feeling up to doing much—band practice included.

So where does this idiom come from? The ocean! Centuries ago, ocean travel was an important way of getting from one place to another. Passengers often spent days or weeks aboard a ship. In all that time, they were bound to hit some bad weather. Storms kicked up big waves and made for a rocky ride. Passengers got tossed back and forth. Many of them got seasick.

Seasick passengers had two choices. Some of them rushed to the rails, where they held on tight as they lost their lunch. Others hurried below deck to the lowest part of the ship. That was where the motion of the ocean was least noticeable. The sick passengers were literally taking shelter underneath the weather that was battering the ship's upper decks.

7

GET IT OUT of YOUR SYSTEM

Samir and his friends were shouting and laughing as his mom drove them to the library. They were busy making rude sound effects as the car pulled into a parking spot.

"OK, boys, we're here," said Samir's mom. "Why don't you all go ahead and get the sound effects out of your systems right now."

The boys all made the loudest and grossest sound effects that they could come up with. With a final laugh, they quieted down and headed into the library.

What do rude noises have to do with any system? And how does making them get anything out of it? Simple. **When you get something out of your system, you're doing something so that you don't feel the need to do it later.**

These boys have lots of energy to get out of their systems before they head back to class!

Maybe you feel the need to jump or run before sitting down for a big test. You can't do it during the test, so you're getting the urge out of your system.

Where does this saying come from? Think about it. Imagine you ate some bad food. Your stomach feels like it's about to do a backflip. What's the best way to get that bad food—and that bad feeling—out of your digestive system? You got it. It's upchuck time. So come to think of it, maybe rude noises really do have something to do with getting it out of your system!

You might get very well acquainted with a toilet if you need to get bad food out of your system. Gross but true.

BITE the BULLET

"My tooth hurts," Juan told his dad. "I can't even chew on one side of my mouth."

"Juan, I think it's time I take you to the dentist," Juan's dad replied. "I know you really didn't want to go last week when your tooth first started hurting. But since the soreness hasn't gone away, we'd better go see Dr. Miller."

"Yeah," Juan said with a sigh. "I hate going to the dentist, but I guess I'll have to bite the bullet this time."

What is Juan talking about? Is biting the bullet some new sort of dental procedure? Maybe it's a weird way to cure a toothache. But what kind of bullet does one have to bite?

Don't worry—Juan won't actually be biting any bullets. **The phrase *bite the bullet* is just a way of saying that one has to do something unpleasant.** When you bite the bullet, you're going ahead with something that's necessary but that you really don't want to do.

Where does this expression come from? Centuries ago, medics had to operate on hurt soldiers during wartime without any painkilling drugs. Painkilling drugs hadn't been invented yet—and that includes the drugs that doctors use today to put people to sleep during surgery. People who go through surgery when they're awake are at risk of biting or swallowing their own tongues. To keep the soldiers from doing that, medics gave them pieces of wood or leather to bite down on. If there was no wood or leather around, a bullet sometimes had to do!

This kid's biting the bullet and visiting the dentist. At least he didn't have to go to the doctor many centuries ago, before painkilling drugs had been invented!

A TASTE of Your OWN MEDICINE

Liz was standing outside the school when her sister, Mikayla, called her on her cell phone. "Did you take my coat?" asked Mikayla. "I was planning to wear that tonight!"

If you nab your sister's coat after she took your shoes, you're giving her a taste of her own medicine.

"**W**ell, yesterday you wore my new shoes to school," Liz barked. "Now I'm giving you a taste of your own medicine!"

Hmm…coats, shoes, and medicine? What could these three things possibly have in common? It's one thing to borrow somebody's clothing but to take that person's medicine? We all know that's just wrong—not to mention dangerous.

Of course, nobody's actually tasting any medicine in this scene. **The expression *a taste of your own medicine* is a way of saying that one person is doing to another what that person had done to someone else in the past.** So if you break plans with a friend to hang out with another friend instead and then that friend cancels on *you*, you've just been given a taste of your own medicine!

This expression probably comes from an old fable. The fable tells of a sketchy guy who sells fake medicine to people, knowing full well that the medicine doesn't really cure anything. But then the sketchy guy gets sick. The people try to nurse him back to health using his own good-for-nothing medicine! Now that's *really* a taste of his own medicine.

KEEP a COLD at BAY

"I don't want to drink my orange juice," Abby complained to her mom. Her mom nudged the glass a little closer.

"Just take a sip or two," she said. "You're coming down with a cold, and orange juice is full of vitamin C. Vitamin C might help you keep that cold at bay."

What is Abby's mom talking about? Keep a cold at bay? How do you keep a cold anywhere—other than in your nose, throat, and lungs? And what in the world is a bay?

The phrase *keep a cold at bay* is a way of saying that you're keeping the cold from really taking hold. You're helping your body fight it off so the cold doesn't make you feel very sick.

Orange juice just may keep you from getting really sick if you're coming down with a head cold.

So how did this idiom get started? We have to go way back to ancient Greece to find out. The ancient Greeks thought that bay trees had almost magical protective powers. Greeks caught outside during a bad storm would huddle under a bay tree to stay safe. Greek soldiers would wear symbols of the bay tree for protection. They were trying to "keep the enemy at bay." Over time, the idea of keeping something at bay grew to include almost anything bad. In modern times, it's most often used to refer to colds and other illnesses. Of course, the bay tree doesn't really provide any protection from colds. If it did, Abby's mom might be asking her to eat a bay leaf instead of drinking her OJ!

Does this bay tree look magical to you?

RUB SALT in the WOUND

Abdul sighed and stared at the floor when his dad asked him how his basketball team had done. "We lost by thirty points," he mumbled.

"And Abdul missed all ten shots he took!" added his little sister, Jala, with a giggle.

"Come on now, Jala," scolded their dad. "Don't rub salt in the wound."

So wait a second—did Abdul miss all those shots because he was wounded? Because that seems like a pretty good excuse. Rubbing salt in the wound doesn't seem like it would do a lot of good, though. In fact, it would hurt—a lot!

If a team really gloats after beating another team, you might say they're rubbing salt in the losing team's wound.

Abdul isn't actually wounded. And no one really put any salt on him. **The phrase *rub salt in the wound* just means that you're making a bad situation even worse for someone.**

This idiom came about centuries ago. Back then, the medical treatments we have now didn't exist. An open wound could easily become infected. That was bad news. An infection might lead to someone having to get his or her limb cut off. It might even lead to death. <u>One way to keep an infection from starting was to rub salt in the wound. The salt would kill harmful bacteria that caused infections.</u> But rubbing salt in a wound would also hurt like crazy. Even though it was done to help a person, it made that person hurt a whole lot more—at least in the short term.

Salt is pretty much the last thing you want rubbed in an open wound.

A CLEAN BILL of HEALTH

Asha was super nervous. She was supposed to leave for her vacation to Florida in two days, but she was afraid she might have strep throat. A ton of kids in her class had had it. Her mom had taken her to the doctor for a strep test to make sure that she was healthy. If she wasn't, Asha's big trip might be off.

Finally, the phone rang. Asha's mom answered. The conversation seemed to last forever. When it was over at last, her mom turned to her and said, "Good news, Asha. You don't have strep. You have a clean bill of health. Start packing for Florida!"

Asha gave a whoop. She was *thrilled* she didn't have strep! But what did her mom mean that she had a clean bill of health? What was a bill? And what did it have to do with health, anyway?

Once again, we have to look to the ships of centuries past for the answer. When a ship came into port, a doctor would board the ship to check everyone on it for signs of disease. If even one passenger had a serious disease such as cholera or the plague, the entire ship had to go back to where it came from. None of the passengers were allowed to get off at the port. If they did, they might spread the disease. If the doctor found no sign of disease, he would create a document—called a bill—that said the ship was clean. So *a clean bill of health* meant that a ship was disease free. Over time, the expression came to refer to a healthy individual rather than a whole ship full of people.

Disease spread quickly on ships that sailed the seas. Here, ship passengers get shots in 1881.

ACHILLES' HEEL

"How'd you do on your math test?" Katie asked Liu.

"Don't ask," Liu answered with disgust. "Multiplication and most division problems give me no trouble at all. But this long division we've been studying lately is really my Achilles' heel."

Achilles' heel? You're supposed to use your head to figure out math problems, not your feet! Feet are great for walking on—but when it comes to doing long division, they're really not much help.

Is Liu *really* trying to use her heels to help her out in math? Of course not. Liu's just saying that long division is her one weakness in math class. **That's all an Achilles' heel is—something that gives you trouble.**

Thetis, the mother of Achilles, dips him in the River Styx. She wanted to give him the ability to live forever.

This expression comes from the myth of Achilles. Achilles was a great warrior of ancient Greece. According to the myth, his mother dipped him in the River Styx. This gave him the power of immortality. (That means he'd never die.) But his mom held onto his heel when she dunked him in the water. His heel never touched the magical river. It was the only part of his body that stayed mortal. Later, in the Trojan War, an arrow struck Achilles in the heel. The arrow killed him. And that's how this expression was born.

KICK the BUCKET

"I haven't seen your warrior character online lately," Luke said to Peter as they ate their lunch. They loved to talk about their adventures on the newest online fantasy game. "Haven't you been playing?"

"I had to start a new character," Peter answered. "I tried to fight a dragon, and my warrior kicked the bucket."

So are we talking about a *magic* bucket here? What sort of special powers does it have? When you kick it, does it shoot flames or freeze the enemy or something?

Sadly, Peter's warrior didn't have a magic bucket. **Kick the bucket is just a way of saying that someone or something died.** Still, that seems like an odd way of putting it. Where does this expression come from?

It's frustrating when your character kicks the bucket when you're gaming!

The truth is, no one is sure. There are several possible explanations. <u>Some people think it refers to an old children's game that ended when a player literally kicked a bucket.</u> Another explanation comes from the slaughtering of pigs centuries ago. When a pig was to be slaughtered, it was hung from a high crossbeam so that all the blood would run out of it. The French word for that beam was *buchet*—which sounds a lot like bucket. As you might imagine, a pig strung up would kick out in panic. When it kicked the *buchet*, the pig was as good as dead. As grim as that sounds, it may well be the real explanation.

WARTS and ALL

Tessa watched as her older brother washed and waxed his new car. Well, it wasn't really new. It was twenty years old, with rusty fenders and a cracked windshield.

"Why do you spend so much time washing that thing?" she asked. "It looks like it might fall apart at any moment."

Jason flashed her a smile. "It's my first car. I love it, warts and all."

A little rust doesn't sound so bad, but a car with warts on it? How does that even work? Of course, there aren't any real warts. **If you say that you love something, *warts and all*, it means that you love every part of it, even its flaws.**

This car might not look too pretty, but its owner loves it warts and all.

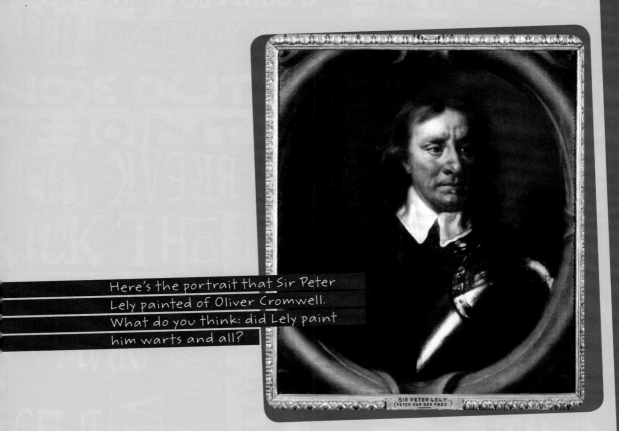

Here's the portrait that Sir Peter Lely painted of Oliver Cromwell. What do you think: did Lely paint him warts and all?

SIR PETER LELY
(PETER VAN DER FAES)

Regardless, that seems like a funny way to describe a car—or anything besides a person with lots of warts. So where does this expression come from? In the 1600s, Oliver Cromwell was the head of the government of England, Scotland, and Ireland. He was having his portrait painted by an artist named Sir Peter Lely. <u>Lely had a reputation for painting portraits intended to flatter the subject. In other words, he left out unattractive features such as warts.</u> But that's not what Cromwell wanted for his portrait. According to some sources, Cromwell told Lely, "Paint my picture truly like me, and not flatter me at all; but remark all these roughnesses, pimples, warts and everything as you see me." In other words, Cromwell wanted a portrait of himself, *warts and all*.

BREAK a LEG

Kendra was so nervous she was almost shaking. It was almost time for her solo performance in the school musical. Hundreds of people would be watching.

"OK, you're up," said her friend Sara backstage. "You can do it. Now get out there and break a leg!"

Whoa … wait a second here. This all seemed nice and friendly until that last part. *Break a leg?* What a horrible thing to tell someone! What's the deal? What kind of friend is this Sara?

Don't get upset with Sara. Obviously, she didn't really want Kendra to fracture

Telling someone to break a leg may not seem very nice—but really this saying only means that you wish the person luck onstage!

any bones. **In showbiz, the expression *break a leg* is just a funny way of saying good luck.**

So in a world of strange idioms, this may seem like one of the strangest. Why do we use such a negative-sounding expression to wish someone luck? It's really a bit of a mystery. Nobody can say for sure exactly where it started. The most widely accepted idea is that years ago, actors thought that telling one another "good luck" would actually bring bad luck. So instead, they said the opposite—"I hope you break a leg." Over time, the expression was shortened, and it's been used ever since.

Real broken legs are no fun at all. You wouldn't wish one on anybody. The good news is that casts and crutches help broken legs heal in a hurry.

NOSE out of JOINT

Teresa and Jade were walking together down the hall when they saw Andrea coming. Teresa waved and motioned for her to join them but got only a scowl in return.

"Oh, don't worry about her," Jade said. "She found out we went to the movies without her last weekend, and now she's got her nose out of joint."

Say what? How on Earth could missing a movie cause an injury to Andrea's nose? And come to think of it, does the nose even *have* any joints?

No, noses don't have joints—and not being invited to a movie obviously can't hurt your nose. **Nose out of joint is just an expression that means someone is offended or upset about something.** Andrea's mad at her friends because she felt left out.

This expression has been used since at least the late 1500s. It most likely comes from the dirty look or scowl people might give when they're angry or upset. That scowl might make their faces look kind of crooked—as if their noses aren't quite straight. The best cure for this imaginary injury is almost always a simple apology!

The girl on the left has her nose out of joint. She feels left out because she wasn't invited to the movies with her friends.

Glossary

bacteria: microscopic living things that exist all around you and inside you. Many bacteria are useful, but some cause disease.

cholera: a deadly infection of the small intestine

idiom: a commonly used expression or phrase that means something different from what it appears to mean

immortality: living forever

medic: someone who is trained to give medical treatment to soldiers

mortal: unable to live forever

plague: a very serious disease that spreads quickly to many people and often causes death

portrait: a painting or other image of a person

slaughter: to kill an animal for its meat

vigor: health and physical strength

vim: energy

wound: an injury

Source Note

25 The Phrase Finder, 2012, http://www.phrases.org.uk/meanings/warts-and-all.html (May 15, 2012).

Further Reading

Amoroso, Cynthia. *I'm All Thumbs!: (And Other Odd Things We Say).* Mankato, MN: Child's World, 2011. Learn more about some of the English language's strangest idioms, and find out why we say the things we say.

Atkinson, Mary. *What Do You Mean?: Communication Isn't Easy.* New York: Children's Press, 2007. Learn about all sorts of things that can confuse communication, from idioms to changing word meanings to slang and different pronunciations.

Doeden, Matt. *Stick Out Like a Sore Thumb: And Other Expressions about Body Parts.* Minneapolis: Lerner Publications Company, 2013. Brush up on thirteen fun and interesting idioms about body parts, from *put your foot in your mouth* to *costs an arm and a leg.*

The Idiom Connection
http://www.idiomconnection.com
The Idiom Connection has tons of easy-to-search explanations of the most common English idioms. Search alphabetically or by theme.

Idiom Site
http://www.idiomsite.com
Check out this website for an alphabetical list of expressions and what they mean.

Moses, Will. *Raining Cats and Dogs.* New York: Philomel Books, 2008. This book offers a humorous approach to investigating idioms and what they really mean.

Paint by Idioms
http://www.funbrain.com/idioms
Check out this simple game. Answer questions about common idioms and watch as a funny picture is painted with every correct answer.

Terban, Marvin. *In a Pickle: And Other Funny Idioms.* New York: Clarion Books, 2007. Through lively text and illustrations, Terban investigates thirty strange expressions, including *in a pickle* and *cry over spilled milk.*

Walton, Rick. *Why the Banana Split: An Adventure in Idioms.* Salt Lake City: Gibbs Smith, 2011. In this fictional story, Walton pokes fun at strange expressions as he tells the tale of a town threatened by a fruit-eating *Tyrannosaurus rex.*

LERNER
e
SOURCE

Expand learning beyond the printed book. Download free, complementary educational resources for this book from our website, www.lernerresource.com.

Index

Photo Acknowledgments

The images in this book are used with the permission of: © Photononstop/
SuperStock, pp. 4, 27; © age fotostock/SuperStock, p. 5; © Richard Levine/Alamy,
p. 6; © Thomas Wiewandt/Taxi/Getty Images, p. 7; © Photo and Co/Lifesize/
Getty Images, p. 8; © Timbrk/Dreamstime.com, p. 9; © Dan Bannister/SuperStock,
p. 11; © iStockphoto.com/Imgorthand, p. 12; © iStockphoto.com/Jill Fromer, p. 13;
© Boccabella Debbie/Oredia Eurl/SuperStock, p. 14; © Gerth Roland/Prisma/
SuperStock, p. 15; © Fuse/Getty Images, p. 16; © iStockphoto.com/Bob Ingelhart,
p. 17; © Culver Pictures, Inc./SuperStock, p. 19; © Asia Images Group/Getty
Images, p. 20; © Alfredo Dagli Orti/The Art Archive at Art Resource, NY, p. 21;
© Kathleen Smith/Alamy, p. 23; © Jason Langley/age fotostock/SuperStock, p. 24;
© Scala/Art Resource, NY, p. 25; © Andersen Ross/Blend Images/Getty Images,
p. 26; © SuperStock/SuperStock, p. 29.

Front cover: © iStockphoto.com/ZoneCreative (foreground); © Versh/
Dreamstime.com (background).

Main body text set in Adrianna Light 11/17.
Typeface provided by Chank.